The Seven

HABITS

Of

EXTREMELY

PRODUCTIVE

PEOPLE

BY

MILTON E. MORGAN

Contents

INTRODUCTION 4

CHAPTER ONE...7

   THE CONCEPT OF BEING PRODUCTIVE 7

CHAPTER TWO 14

   CONNECT THEIR BEHAVIORS WITH THEIR
GOALS...14

CHAPTER THREE 22

   CONCENTRATE ON THE CONSEQUENCES OF
THEIR ACTIONS...22

CHAPTER FOUR 28

   OPTIMIZE THEIR EFFICIENCY 28

CHAPTER FIVE 36

   THINK WINWIN SITUATIONS 36

CHAPTER SIX..45

   UNDERSTAND TO BE UNDERSTOOD 45

CHAPTER SEVEN 53

   SYNERGIZE 53

CHAPTER EIGHT 61

   SEEK FEEDBACK AND IMPROVE 61

CHAPTER NINE 66

   FREQUENTLY ASKED QUESTIONS 66

CONCLUSION..75

INTRODUCTION

Have you ever wondered why some people seem to accomplish so much in a day while others struggle to complete their tasks? How do they efficiently manage their time, energy, and resources? What are their productivity secrets?

If you want to know the answers to these questions, this book is for you. In this book, I will discuss the seven habits of highly productive people and how you can use them in your own life. These behaviors are founded on research and practice rather than theories or beliefs. They apply not only to your professional life, but also to your personal and social life. They are concepts and mindsets that can improve your productivity, not just tips or tactics.

You may be asking what distinguishes this book from other productivity books. There are three major differences. First and foremost, this book is about accomplishing better rather than more. It is not a matter of squeezing more work into your calendar, but of selecting the proper tasks and performing them well. Working smarter rather than harder is the goal. Second, this book is about establishing a flexible framework rather than adhering to a strict structure. It is not a case of imposing a one size fits all approach, but rather of tailoring to your specific situation and preferences. It is not a matter of obeying rules, but of developing habits. Third, this book is not about productivity for the sake of productivity, but rather about productivity with a purpose. Being effective is more important than being busy. It is not about achieving more, but rather about achieving what is important.

You might be wondering why I wrote this book. So, this book has a personal tale and motivation for me. I used to be a pretty inefficient person. I was constantly procrastinating, getting distracted, and feeling overwhelmed. I lacked defined goals, focus, and a sense of accomplishment. I was frustrated, anxious, and dissatisfied. I wanted to change, but I had no idea how. I tried several productivity books, classes, and applications, but none of them worked for me. They were either overly intricate, uninteresting, or impractical. I felt as if I was squandering my time and money.

Then I learned about the seven habits of highly productive people. They came from a variety of sources, including books, articles, podcasts, films, and interviews. I researched, practiced, and perfected them. I used them in my own life and noticed incredible benefits. I improved my focus, organization, and efficiency. I exceeded my objectives, added more value, and made a greater effect. I lowered my stress, boosted my happiness, and strengthened my connections. I become a more productive and better person as a result of this experience.

I chose to write this book in order to share these habits with you and to assist you in being more productive as well. Productivity, in my opinion, is a skill rather than a talent. It is something you can learn rather than something you are born with. It is something you do rather than something you have. And it's something you can start doing right now.

I hope you enjoy reading this book and find it useful and useful. I hope you learn and adopt the seven habits of extraordinarily productive people in your own life. I wish you become more productive and achieve what is important to you.

CHAPTER ONE
THE CONCEPT OF BEING PRODUCTIVE
What exactly is productivity, and why is it important?

Productivity is a measure of how well you use your resources to achieve your objectives. It is not simply about achieving more in less time, but also about doing the right things in the best way possible. Productivity is vital not just for your professional life, but also for your personal and social life. It can aid in the enhancement of your performance, satisfaction, and wellbeing.

Being productive has numerous advantages, including:

You can accomplish more with less work and expense. You may boost output and quality while decreasing input and errors by optimizing your processes, minimizing waste, and focusing on value. According to one study, employees who work from home are 52% less likely to take time off6.

You'll have more time and energy for other things. You may do your work faster and easier if you manage your time, prioritize your duties, and avoid distractions. This can allow you to devote more time and energy to your interests, family, and friends. According to one survey, 86% of employees prefer to work alone to prevent interruptions6.

 You can improve your reputation and earnings. You may wow your clients, stakeholders, and co-workers by producing exceptional outcomes, exceeding expectations, and making an impact. This can improve your reputation, recognition, and earnings. According to one projection, the average revenue per employee of the world's top ten most productive corporations in 2020 will be $1.8 million.

However, there are numerous disadvantages to being **unproductive**, such as:

You can waste time and money on activities that are unneeded or of little value. You can waste time and money by using inefficient or obsolete procedures, performing redundant or irrelevant work, or devoting too much effort to unimportant problems. According to one analysis, the cost of ineffective meetings in the United States in 2019 was expected to be $399 billion.

You may feel stressed and frustrated. You may feel overwhelmed, nervous, or furious if you have too much work, not enough time, or too many interruptions. This can have an impact on your mood, health, and relationships. In 2020, for example, 71% of employees reported feeling worried or burned out at work, according to a survey.

It is possible to overlook opportunities and fall behind. Failure to mcct dcadlines, please customers, or achieve goals can result in the loss of a competitive advantage, market share, or career opportunities. This might have a negative impact on your credibility, confidence, and progress. According to one research, the productivity gap between the top and lowest 25% of enterprises in the United States was 3.1 times in 2018.

As you can see, productivity is an important component in determining your success and happiness. It can have a significant impact on your performance and outcomes. That is why you must learn and adopt the seven habits of highly productive people, which we will cover in the next chapters.

Before we go on to the next chapters, I'd want to introduce you to a basic but effective framework for understanding and using the seven habits of highly productive people. The PIE framework (Purpose, Impact, and Efficiency) is what I call it.

The PIE paradigm is built on the premise that productivity is about doing better, not merely doing more. Quality is more important than quantity. It is not just about intake but also about output. It is not only about activity, but also about outcomes.

The PIE framework is made up of three parts:

Purpose: The why behind your actions. It is the cause, meaning, and significance for what you do. Your decisions are guided by your goals, vision, and mission. Your activities are driven by motivation, passion, and inspiration.

Impact: This is what your actions will have. It is the result, effect, and consequence of your actions. Your performance is measured by the aim, objective, and target. It is the worth, advantage, and distinction that you generate for yourself and others.

Efficiency: This is how your actions are carried out. It is the technique, process, and system by which you do things. Your resources are optimized by your plan, strategy, and tactics. You control and increase the pace, quality, and cost.

The PIE framework can assist you in three ways to increase productivity:

For starters, it can assist you in aligning your behaviors with your mission. You can prioritize your efforts, overcome distractions, and stay motivated if you have a clear and important goal. You can also share your goal with others and get their support and criticism. This is the first habit of highly productive people, which we shall go into in depth in Chapter 2.

Second, it might assist you in focusing on the consequences of your actions. You may achieve your goals, optimize your resources, and avoid wasting time by measuring and maximizing the impact of your actions. You can also examine the impact of your actions on others and make changes as needed. This is the second habit of highly productive people, which we will go over in depth in Chapter 3.

Third, it can assist you in optimizing your efficiency. You may get more done in less time, reduce stress, and improve the quality of your job by increasing your efficiency. You can also improve your operations by learning from your efficiency. This is the third habit of highly productive people, which we shall go over in depth in Chapter 4.

The PIE framework is a basic but effective method for increasing productivity. It can assist you in doing the right things in the greatest possible way for the right reasons. It can help you achieve better rather than more. It can help you achieve what is important, not just what is urgent or simple.

In the following chapters, we will go over each component of the PIE framework in detail and show you how to use them in your daily life. We will also study the other four habits of extraordinarily productive people, which are founded on but go beyond the PIE framework.

These habits can help you improve your productivity as an individual, as well as a team player, leader, and learner. They will assist you in creating value for yourself as well as others. They will assist you in developing not just as a professional but also as a person.

Are you prepared to study and implement the seven habits of highly productive people?

CHAPTER TWO
CONNECT THEIR BEHAVIORS
WITH THEIR GOALS

The first habit of highly productive people is to connect their behaviors with their goals. This implies that you have a clear and meaningful purpose for what you do and that you act in accordance with your reason. As we learned in the previous chapter, your mission is the why behind your activities.

What is the significance of having a purpose for your productivity? There are three basic causes for this:

Having a goal in mind will help you prioritize your efforts. When you have a goal, you can readily distinguish between what is significant and what is not. You can concentrate on things that are relevant to your goal and disregard or delegate those that are not. You can also track your progress and outcomes by setting SMART goals (Specific, Measurable, Achievable, Relevant, and Time-bound) that are drawn from your purpose. For example, if your goal is to assist people better their health, you might prioritize tasks that contribute directly or indirectly to that goal, such as writing a blog post, making a video, or leading a workshop. You may also measure your influence and feedback by setting SMART goals, such as reaching 10,000 subscribers, generating 100 views, or having 20 participants.

Having a goal in mind can help you overcome distractions. When you have a goal in mind, it is much easier to avoid the temptations and interruptions that can derail your productivity. You may avoid procrastination and multitasking by remaining focused and devoted to your tasks. You can also utilize tools and tactics to eliminate or reduce distractions, such as banning apps, turning off notifications, or wearing headphones. For example, if your goal is to assist people better their health, you can resist distractions that may keep you from completing your work, such as social media, email, or watching TV. You can also utilize tools and tactics to create a distraction-free atmosphere for your work, such as banning apps, turning off notifications, or wearing headphones.

Having a goal in mind can help you stay motivated. When you have a goal, it is much easier to locate the intrinsic and extrinsic rewards that will keep you motivated. You can discover joy and fulfilment in your tasks, as well as purpose and value in reaching your objectives. Affirmations, visualizations, and rewards are some tools and approaches that might help you enhance your motivation. For example, if your goal is to assist people better their health, the delight and satisfaction of sharing your knowledge and abilities, as well as the meaning and worth of making a positive difference in people's lives, can keep you motivated. You can also utilize tools and strategies to strengthen your drive and celebrate your accomplishments, such as affirmations, visualizations, or prizes.

As you can see, having a purpose can assist you in becoming more productive by assisting you in prioritizing your duties, overcoming distractions, and remaining motivated. But how can you discover and clarify your purpose?

Here are some practises to get you started:

Create a personal mission statement. A personal mission statement is a brief and compelling statement that encapsulates your purpose, values, and aspirations. It can aid in the definition of who you are, what you do, and why you do it. To create your personal mission statement, utilize the following formula: I assist (who) by (how). For example, your personal mission statement could be: I assist people in improving their health by giving practical, evidence-based information and assistance.

List your core values. The concepts and beliefs that influence your behaviors and decisions are known as your core values. They can assist you in aligning your behaviors with your mission and avoiding actions that are counter to your purpose. To write down your essential values, follow these steps: 1) Create a list of terms that reflect what is important to you, such as honesty, creativity, or compassion. 2) Narrow your list down to the top five words that speak to you the most. 3) Explain what each phrase means to you and how you use it in your daily life. Your basic values could include, for example, honesty: I always speak the truth, and I expect others to do the same. Creativity: I am constantly looking for new and better ways to accomplish things, and I urge others to do the same. Compassion: I am always concerned about the wellbeing of others and attempt to assist them whenever possible.

Make a list of your SMART goals.

Your SMART goals are the objectives that you want to achieve that are specific, measurable, achievable, relevant, and time-bound. They may assist you in translating your purpose into action as well as measuring your progress and achievements.

To write down your SMART goals, follow these steps:

- Determine what you want to achieve and why it is essential to you.
- Ensure that your objective is specific, measurable, attainable, meaningful, and time-bound.
- Divide your goal into smaller, more doable segments, and give dates and resources to each one.
- Review and revise your aim on a frequent basis. Your SMART goal could be, for example, "I want to reach 10,000 subscribers on my health blog by the end of the year because it will help me spread my message and impact more people." To accomplish this objective, I will do the following:

1) Write and publish one blog post per week, and share it on social media and via email.

2) Make and upload one video per month, linking it to my blog and social media accounts.

3) Hold one online workshop per quarter and invite my subscribers and followers to attend. Join.

4) Track and analyse my traffic, interaction, and feedback to better my content and approach.

These activities and recommendations can help you discover and clarify your mission, as well as connect your behaviors with it. This allows you to be more productive and achieve what is important to you and others. This is the initial habit of highly productive people, and it serves as the foundation for the PIE framework.

Write a letter to yourself in the future. Consider yourself in five or 10 years, living a life that is in alignment with your mission. What exactly are you doing? What are your thoughts? What have you achieved? Write a letter to your future self in which you describe your perfect existence and how you arrived there. This can assist you in visualizing your goal and developing a strategy for accomplishing it.

Make a vision board. A vision board is an image, word, and symbol collage that represents your purpose, aspirations, and dreams. To make your vision board, you can use magazines, newspapers, online sources, or your own artwork. You can also include inspirational quotations, affirmations, or questions. Display your vision board somewhere you can see it every day as a reminder and motivator to follow through on your goals.

Seek feedback from others. It can be difficult to identify your purpose on your own at times. You might require some outside input or affirmation from those who know you well or share your interests. You can ask them, for example, "What do you think I'm good at?" What do you think I'm interested in? What do you think I can offer the world? How do you believe I can improve? With an open mind, consider their critique and use it as a source of knowledge and encouragement.

Try out different activities. Sometimes the greatest method to discover your purpose is to experiment with various activities and see what piques your interest and passion. Join a club, take a class, volunteer for a good cause, or start a project that interests you. You might learn a new skill, a new pastime, or a new way to serve others. You might also meet new people who can help you or push you to grow. Experimenting with various things can help you broaden your horizons and discover your expertise.

CHAPTER THREE
CONCENTRATE ON THE CONSEQUENCES OF THEIR ACTIONS

The second habit of highly productive people is to concentrate on the consequences of their actions. This implies that you consider the end, effect, and consequence of your actions, and that you take actions that have a positive and meaningful impact.

Why is it vital to focus on the impact for your productivity?

There are three basic causes for this:

Concentrating on the impact can help you reach your objectives. When you concentrate on the impact, it is much easier to connect your actions with your goals and to track your progress and results. You can also assess your performance and determine your strong points and weak points. You can also utilize tools and approaches like the OKR (Objectives and Key Results) framework, the GROW (Goal, Reality, Options, Will) model, or the SMARTER (Specific, Measurable, Achievable, Relevant, Time-bound, Evaluate, Revise) criteria to help you develop and achieve SMART goals.

Paying attention to the impact can help you optimize your resources. When you concentrate on the impact, you can simply prioritize your projects based on their importance and urgency, allocating your time, energy, and money accordingly. You can also delete or reduce tasks with little or no impact, and avoid overcommitting or under-delivering. You can also use tools and techniques like the Eisenhower matrix, the Pareto principle, or Parkinson's Law to help you optimize your resources.

Paying attention to the impact can assist you avoid wasting time. When you concentrate on the impact, you will find it easier to resist the temptations and interruptions that can divert your attention away from your activities and prevent procrastination and perfectionism. You can also employ timesaving tools and strategies such as the Pomodoro technique, the Kanban board, or the Getting Things Done (GTD) method.

As you can see, concentrating on the impact can help you become more productive by assisting you in meeting your objectives, optimizing your resources, and avoiding time waste. However, how can you quantify and maximize the impact of your actions?

Here are magnificent ways to get you started:

Make a list of your important findings. Your key results are concrete, measurable, and time-bound indicators of how effectively you are meeting your goals. They can assist you with quantifying and qualifying the impact of your efforts, as well as tracking your progress and results. You can use the following steps to write down your important results:

- Identify your objective and ensure it is clear, useful, and relevant.
- Determine the important findings that will demonstrate that you have met your goal, and ensure that they are specific, quantitative, and time-bound.
- Use numbers, percentages, or ratings to record your main results, and assign each one a target and a deadline.
  If your goal is to increase blog traffic, for example, your key results could be:
- Increase the number of visitors by 50% at the end of the month.
- By the end of the month, increase the average time on page by 20%.
- By the end of the month, increase the bounce rate by 10%.

Create an impact statement. Your impact statement is a brief but strong statement that outlines the worth, benefit, and difference you make for yourself and others. It can assist you in communicating and demonstrating the impact of your efforts, as well as receiving feedback and appreciation. You can compose your impact statement using the following formula: I aid (who) to (what) by (how). For example, your impact statement could be: On my blog, I assist individuals improve their health by providing them with practical, evidence-based information and recommendations.

Seek feedback from others. It can be difficult to assess the influence of your activities on your own at times. You may require some outside input or validation from those who are affected or interested in your actions. You can ask them things like, "What do you think about my actions?" What impact do they have on you or others? What are the advantages and disadvantages of my actions? How can I make my acts or their impact more effective? With an open mind, listen to their critique and use it as a source of insight and progress.

Experiment with various actions. Sometimes, experimenting with multiple approaches to determine what works and what doesn't is the greatest method to optimize the impact of your efforts. You can experiment with various actions, tactics, or strategies and assess their impact using your key outcomes. You can also compare and contrast several acts to see which have the most positive and substantial impact. Experimenting with various activities can assist you in optimizing your impact and learning from your experience.

These exercises and recommendations can assist you in measuring and optimizing the impact of your activities, as well as focusing on the impact of your actions. This allows you to be more productive and achieve what is important to you and others. This is the second habit of highly productive people, as well as the second component of the PIE framework.

The third habit of incredibly productive people is to optimize your efficiency, which we shall explore in the next chapter. We'll study how to increase your efficiency and how to use tools and approaches to accomplish so. Keep an eye out!

CHAPTER FOUR
OPTIMIZE THEIR EFFICIENCY

The third habit of highly productive people is to optimize their efficiency. This means that you make the best use of your resources, such as time, energy, and money, to reach your objectives. As we established in the last chapter, your efficiency is the how of your actions.

Why is increasing your efficiency vital for increasing your productivity?

There are three basic causes for this:

Improving your efficiency will help you accomplish more in less time. When you improve your efficiency, you can boost production and quality while decreasing input and errors. You can also accomplish more in less time, freeing you more time for other things. You can also utilize tools and strategies like the Pomodoro technique, the Kanban board, or the Getting Things Done (GTD) method to help you get more done in less time.

Improving your efficiency can assist you in reducing stress. When you enhance your efficiency, you can reduce your workload and stress while also improving your work-life balance. You can also avoid or manage frequent stressors like deadlines, interruptions, or disagreements. You can also utilize stress-reduction methods and strategies such as meditation, exercise, or music.

Improving your efficiency can assist you increase your work quality. When you maximize your efficiency, you can improve your abilities, knowledge, and habits while also producing exceptional results. You can also boost your reputation, notoriety, and earnings. You can also employ tools and approaches to improve your work quality, such as feedback, coaching, or learning.

As you can see, improving your efficiency can help you become more productive by allowing you to get more done in less time, reduce stress, and enhance your job quality. But how can you improve your productivity?

Here are some methods and best practices to consider:

Make a work plan. Planning your job can help you maximize your efficiency by defining and organizing your goals, tasks, and resources in a logical and realistic manner. Planning your work can also assist you in anticipating and preventing any problems, as well as adjusting your strategy as needed.

Observe these stages

- Identify your goal and make sure it is SMART (Specific, Measurable, Achievable, Relevant, and Time-bound).
- Divide your goal into smaller, more doable activities, and allocate deadlines and resources to each one.
- Use the Eisenhower matrix or the Pareto principle to help you prioritize your tasks based on their importance and urgency.
- Schedule your tasks in your calendar and aid yourself using a project management application or a to-do list.
- Review and revise your plan on a frequent basis.

Group your tasks. Batching your work might help you maximize your efficiency by grouping comparable or related tasks together and completing them in a single session. Batching your work can also assist you avoid switching costs and distractions that can occur while switching between jobs.

To batch your work, follow these steps:

- Identify the tasks that can be grouped together, such as emails, phone calls, or reports.
- Select a time period for each batch, such as morning, afternoon, or evening.
- Use the Pomodoro technique or Parkinson's Law to help you set a timing for each batch.
- Concentrate on one batch at a time, avoiding multitasking and interruptions.
- Take a short break between batches to relax or treat yourself.

Delegate your responsibilities. Delegating your job can help you maximize your efficiency by allowing you to delegate some of your chores to those who have the necessary abilities, time, or interest. Delegating your job can also free up your time and energy for more critical or influential duties, as well as help you strengthen your leadership and collaborative abilities.

To delegate your work, follow these steps:

- Identify duties that can be delegated, such as routine, low-value, or low-skill tasks.

- Select the appropriate individual to delegate to, such as a co-worker, a subordinate, or a freelancer. 3) Clearly and effectively communicate the task, as well as give the essential information, directions, and expectations.
- Monitor and support the individual, offering comments, guidance, and assistance as needed.
- Thank and appreciate the individual, and praise them for their efforts.

Make your work more automated. By utilizing technology or software to conduct parts of your activities automatically or semi-automatically, you can improve your efficiency. You can also save time and money by automating your work, as well as eliminate errors and hazards and boost consistency and reliability.

To automate your work, follow these steps:

- Identify tasks that can be automated, such as repetitive, predictable, or basic chores.
- Select the appropriate technology or program for automating your chores, such as a spreadsheet, script, or app.
- Install and test the tool or software to ensure that it works properly and securely.
- Run and monitor the tool or software, as well as review the results and feedback.
- Update and improve the tool or software, as well as resolve any problems or bugs.

Enhance your abilities. Improving your skills can help you maximize your efficiency by enhancing your knowledge, abilities, and habits, allowing you to accomplish things better and faster. Improving your abilities can also boost your confidence, competence, and creativity.

You can utilize the following stages to develop your talents:

- Identify the skills that you need or wish to improve, such as writing, speaking, or coding.
- Select the most appropriate source or method for learning or practicing your

abilities, such as a book, a course, or a mentor.

- Create a goal and a strategy for skill development that is SMART (Specific, Measurable, Achievable, Relevant, and Time-bound).
- Regularly learn and practice your talents, and use feedback, coaching, or learning to assist you.
- Evaluate and review your skills, as well as track and improve your development.

These methods and best practices can assist you in increasing your efficiency and doing things in the most effective way possible. You can become more productive, get more done in less time, reduce stress, and improve your job quality by doing so. This is the third habit of highly productive people, as well as the third component of the PIE framework.

CHAPTER FIVE
THINK WINWIN SITUATIONS

The fourth habit of highly productive people is to think win-win situations. This means that instead of competing or compromise, you embrace a mindset that seeks mutual benefit and value for yourself and others. You see others as partners, not adversaries or barriers. You seek solutions that meet the needs and interests of everyone, not just your own. Thinking win-win is the inverse of thinking win-lose or lose-lose, which are zero-sum or negative-sum scenarios in which one party's benefit is another's loss or both parties lose.

Why is it vital to think win-win when it comes to productivity?

There are three basic causes for this

Thinking in terms of win-win situations can help you interact more effectively with others. You can develop trust and rapport with your consumers, stakeholders, and co-workers when you think win-win. You can also talk more openly and honestly, as well as listen more actively and compassionately. You can also settle disagreements in a more constructive and creative manner, as well as avoid or manage common conflict causes such as misconceptions, assumptions, or emotions.

Thinking in terms of win-win situations can help you create value for all parties. When you think win-win, you may recognize and exploit each party's talents and resources, resulting in unique and synergistic solutions. You can also discuss and trade information, feedback, and acknowledgement, as well as learn from one another. You can also increase the size of the pie rather than divide it, creating more chances and advantages for everyone.

Thinking in terms of win-win situations can help you achieve your objectives and make an impression. When you think win-win, you may match your goals and influence with the aims and impacts of others, resulting in a shared vision and mission. You may also track your progress and outcomes, as well as measure and maximize the influence of your activities on yourself and others. You can also recognize and appreciate your accomplishments and contributions, as well as inspire and motivate others.

As you can see, thinking win-win can help you become more productive by allowing you to cooperate with people more effectively, generate value for all parties, and realize your goals and influence. But how can you conceive in terms of win-win situations and generate them?

Salary negotiation. Assume you are interviewing for a job and negotiating your compensation with the employer. Demanding a high wage, regardless of the employer's budget or the market rate, is lose-lose strategy. Accepting a low income, regardless of your qualifications or aspirations, would be lose-lose situation. A win-win strategy would be to research the wage range for the position and the industry, and then propose a fair and reasonable salary that reflects your talents and expertise while also meeting the demands and limits of the company. Other components of the remuneration package, including as perks, incentives, or flexible hours, can also be negotiated to bring value to both parties.

Participating in a group project. Assume you are working on a team project and have been assigned various roles and assignments. A lose-lose strategy would be to compete with your co-workers, either outperforming or undermining them. A lose-lose strategy would be to compromise with your teammates and accept a mediocre or inferior result. Cooperating with your teammates and supporting and complementing each other is a win-win situation. You can also interact and coordinate your efforts, as well as provide comments and acknowledgement to one another. You can also seek and generate synergy by combining your thoughts and efforts to get a greater result than any of you could achieve on your own.

The first principle is mutual respect. The core of win-win thinking is mutual respect. It means you treat others as you would like to be treated, and you regard and understand their opinions and feelings.

To demonstrate mutual respect, follow these guidelines:

- Use polite and positive words, and avoid disrespectful or derogatory language.
- Recognize and validate the opposing party's point of view rather than ignoring or disparaging it.
- Express gratitude and appreciation for the input of the other party, rather than taking it for granted or dismissing it.

Empathy is the second principle. The key to thinking win-win is empathy. It implies that you make an effort to comprehend the other party's needs and interests, and that you are concerned about their wellbeing and happiness.

To demonstrate empathy, use the following strategies:

- Ask open-ended questions and listen attentively and actively to the other party's responses.
- Summarize what the other party says and check for comprehension and agreement.
- Express your feelings and emotions, as well as acknowledge and respond to the feelings and emotions of the other party.

Synergy is the third principle. The result of thinking win-win is synergy. It means you create a situation in which the whole is greater than the sum of its parts and you accomplish more together than separately.

- You can use the following tips to create synergy: identify and Use each party's strengths and resources instead of focusing on their faults and limitations.

- Develop and share fresh and inventive ideas rather than settling for traditional or familiar solutions.
- Seek and provide feedback and acknowledgement, as well as learn from one another's experiences and perspectives.

Following on from the ideas of creating win-win situations:

Communication is the fourth principle. Effective communication is required for win-win thinking. It entails openly communicating your own wants and interests while also being open to others' needs and interests. You can effectively communicate by:

Engage in active listening by paying close attention to the speaker, avoiding interruptions, and providing feedback that demonstrates you comprehend their point of view.

Use "I" expressions to express yourself without blaming others or making assumptions about them.

Seek clarification by asking questions if you do not fully comprehend the other party's point of view and confirming that they have also understood your comments.

Adaptability. Being adaptable entails being willing to change your approach in response to new information or changing circumstances. It enables the development of solutions that benefit all parties involved. To be adaptable, you can:

Maintain an open mind to new ideas and solutions that may better achieve the combined goals of all parties.

Be willing to modify your goals and actions in response to feedback and changing circumstances.

Recognize that compromise is often essential, but constantly strive for solutions that benefit everyone.

Creativity is the sixth principle. In win-win thinking, creativity entails exploring beyond the obvious solutions to develop novel ways to produce mutual benefit. You may encourage creativity by doing the following:

Promote brainstorming sessions in which all ideas are welcomed and explored without prejudice.

Seek methods to integrate diverse viewpoints and strengths in order to create new opportunities.

Be willing to challenge the current quo and take measured risks in exchange for the possibility of bigger rewards for all.

By implementing these concepts into your interactions with others, you can build a win-win mindset that not only boosts your productivity but also deepens your relationships and increases your chances of success.

Thinking win-win is a powerful habit that can lead to more productive and peaceful professional and personal relationships. It is about fostering a collaborative culture in which everyone feels appreciated and invested in the outcomes. You may provide the groundwork for long-lasting collaborations and shared achievements by adopting the concepts of mutual respect, empathy, synergy, communication, flexibility, and innovation.

The fifth habit of extraordinarily productive people will be discussed in the NEXT chapter: seek first to understand, then to be understood. This habit will go over the significance of effective communication and comprehension in achieving productivity and success. Keep an eye out for further information on how to boost your productivity through compassionate and strategic communication.

CHAPTER SIX
UNDERSTAND TO BE
UNDERSTOOD

The fifth habit of highly productive people is to want to understand before being understood.

This means you listen to and sympathize with your consumers, stakeholders, and co-workers before communicating with and convincing them. You strive to grasp their wants, expectations, and feelings by seeing things through their eyes. You also attempt to comprehend the environment and circumstances in which they operate, as well as the problems and opportunities they confront.

Why is it necessary for your productivity to seek first to understand, then to be understood?

There are three basic causes for this:

Seeking to understand first, then to be understood, can help you provide better solutions. When you attempt to understand first, you may identify and analyse your customers', stakeholders', and colleagues' problems and aspirations, and create solutions that are tailored and relevant to them. You may also test and validate your solutions, and receive comments and suggestions for improvement from them. You can also employ tools and techniques like the design thinking process, the lean start-up method, or the agile framework to help you produce better solutions.

Seeking to understand first, then to be understood, might assist you in meeting their needs and expectations. When you attempt to understand first, you will be able to find and meet the wants and desires of your consumers, stakeholders, and colleagues, as well as generate value and influence for them. You might also thrill and impress them by exceeding their expectations. You can also utilize tools and strategies like the customer journey map, the value proposition canvas, or the Kano model to help you meet their requirements and expectations.

Seeking first to understand, then to be understood, can aid in dispute resolution. When you endeavour to understand before you act, you can prevent or control typical sources of conflict, such as misconceptions, preconceptions, or emotions. You can also establish common ground and mutual interests, and then negotiate and collaborate to achieve a win-win situation. You can also employ conflict resolution tools and strategies such as the Thomas Kilmann conflict mode instrument, the interest-based relational approach, or the Harvard negotiating method.

As you can see, striving to understand first, then being understood, can help you become more productive by allowing you to give better solutions, satisfy their requirements and expectations, and resolve problems. But how can you want to comprehend before being understood?

Here are some skills and practices that may be useful to you:

The first skill is active listening. Active listening is a critical communication ability that entails taking in information from others and reflecting back to them (in questions and body language) that you heard them.

You can use the following tips to practice active listening:

Pay complete and undivided attention to the speaker. Remove all distractions, judgments, and counterarguments from your thoughts. Avoid the need to interject your own thoughts.

Demonstrate interest by making good eye contact, nodding, and utilizing vocal cues like "uhhuh" or "I see."

Pay attention to (and use) nonverbal indicators including tone of voice, facial expressions, and gestures to grasp the speaker's emotions and attitudes.

Use open-ended inquiries like "What do you mean by that?" or "How did that make you feel?" to elicit additional comments.

Summarize what the speaker stated and check for understanding and agreement by asking questions like "So, what you are saying is..." or "Is that correct?"

Empathic communication. Understanding and sharing the feelings and emotions of others, as well as expressing your own feelings and emotions in a polite and constructive manner, is an important interpersonal skill.

You can utilize the following tips to practice empathic communication:

Use "I" sentences to communicate your thoughts and feelings without blaming or assuming anything about others, such as "I am frustrated when you do not respond to my emails" or "I appreciate your assistance with this project."

Use "you" phrases to acknowledge and validate others' thoughts and feelings without agreeing or disagreeing with them, such as "You appear upset about this situation" or "You did a fantastic job on this task."

Use "we" words to demonstrate that you are on the same team and willing to collaborate to find a solution, such as "We have a common goal here" or "We can figure this out together."

The first method is **The 5 Whys**. The five whys is a problem-solving strategy that involves repeatedly asking "why" to get to the fundamental cause of a problem. It can help you grasp the underlying causes and motivations behind people' and your own actions and behaviors. You can apply the five whys in the following ways3:

State the problem or scenario you wish to comprehend as a question, such as "Why is the customer unhappy with our product?" or "Why am I feeling stressed about this deadline?"

Ask "why?" and respond with information and evidence, such as "Because the product does not meet their expectations" or "Because I have too much work to do."

Ask "why" again and respond based on the prior answer, such as "Because the product has a flaw that affects its performance" or "Because I did not plan my work well."

Repeat the process until you have questioned "why" five times or have found a root cause that you can address or influence, such as "Because the quality control process was not followed properly" or "Because I did not prioritize my tasks based on their value and urgency."

Method two is reflective listening. Reflective listening is a communication method that involves reflecting back to the other person what they are saying and feeling. It ensures that you have accurately understood their message and demonstrates that you are participating in the conversation. You can develop reflective listening by doing the following:

In your own language, repeat or paraphrase the speaker's remarks to demonstrate that you are paying attention and digesting the information.

Reflect the speaker's emotions by acknowledging their feelings, which aids in the development of a stronger relationship and trust.

If you are confused about the speaker's message or intent, ask clarifying questions to urge them to explain and offer you with a deeper understanding.

Nonviolent Communication (NVC) is Method three. Marshall Rosenberg established NVC as a communication approach that focuses on expressing ourselves with clarity and empathy, as well as receiving messages from others with compassion.

NVC has four components: observation, feeling, need, and request. You can utilize NVC in the following ways:

Begin by observing what is going on without analysing or judging it. "When I see that the report is incomplete..." for example.

Explain your reaction to the observation. For instance, "...I am concerned..."

Determine the requirement associated with the emotion. On that note, "...because I need to have all the information to make an informed decision."

Make a specific request for action that addresses the need. Let's say, for example, "...would you be willing to finish the report by tomorrow noon?"

You can dramatically improve your capacity to understand others and be understood in return by mastering these skills and strategies. This practice not only boosts productivity but also promotes a good and collaborative workplace in which everyone's voice is heard and valued.

CHAPTER SEVEN
SYNERGIZE

The sixth habit of highly productive people is to synergize. This means that you use your team's diversity and capabilities to produce new ideas, solve challenging challenges, and achieve better results. You see your team as a source of innovation, learning, and progress, not as a constraint or a cause of competition. You seek solutions that foster synergy, or situations in which the total is greater than the sum of its parts.

What are the benefits of synergizing for your productivity? There are three basic causes for this:

Synergizing can assist you come up with new ideas. When you synergize, you can tap into your team's collective intelligence and wisdom to explore new views and opportunities. You can also inspire and challenge each other, resulting in new insights and breakthroughs. You can also use tools and techniques like brainstorming, mind mapping, or the SCAMPER approach to help you produce new ideas.

Synergizing can assist you in solving complex challenges. Synergy allows you to pool your resources and skills to solve situations that are beyond your own capacities. You can also share and analyze information and data, as well as discover trends and solutions. You can also use tools and strategies like the five whys, the fishbone diagram, or the six thinking caps to help you tackle complex problems.

Synergizing can assist you in achieving bigger achievements. When you collaborate, you may multiply your output and quality while also delivering greater value and impact. You can also encourage and motivate one another, as well as celebrate and respect one another's accomplishments. You can also utilize tools and strategies such as the OKR (Objectives and Key Results) framework, the GROW (Goal, Reality, Options, Will) model, or the SMARTER (Specific, Measurable, Achievable, Relevant, Time-bound, Evaluate, Revise) criteria to help you accomplish better results.

As you can see, synergizing can help you become more productive by assisting you in the generation of novel ideas, the resolution of complex challenges, and the achievement of larger outcomes. But how can you synergize and foster a synergistic culture?

Some principles and practices to consider:

Principle 1: A shared vision. A shared vision is a unified and compelling vision of the future that you and your team wish to build. It can assist you in aligning your goals and actions, as well as inspiring and energizing your team.

You can utilize the following stages to develop a shared vision:

1) Invite your team members to share their personal visions, and then listen to and respect their contributions.

2) Identify and apply the common themes and values that emerge from your team's views as the foundation for your shared vision.

3) Create a clear and succinct statement that encapsulates your shared vision, using colorful and uplifting language.

4) Communicate and exhibit your team's and other stakeholders' common vision, and use it as a guide and reminder for your activities.

 Principle 2: Mutual assistance. Mutual support is the act of assisting and being assisted by your teammates. It can assist you in developing trust and rapport, as well as improving your performance and wellbeing.

You can utilize the following guidelines to provide and accept mutual support:

1) Offer your help to your team members when they need it, and do so truly and respectfully.

 2) When you need support, ask for it honestly and humbly from your team members.

3) Express gratitude and appreciation for the assistance you provide and receive, as well as reward and acknowledge your team members for their assistance.

Principle 3 provide feedback. Feedback is the information and evaluation about your activities and results that you and your team members communicate. It can help you learn and improve, as well as increase the quality and impact of your work.

You can use the following ideas to offer and accept feedback:

- Offer feedback that is specific, timely, and constructive, and focus on the behavior and the outcome rather than the person and the goal.
- Accept open, honest, and courteous critique, and listen and reply with inquiry and appreciation.
- Seek and share feedback on a regular basis, and use it to gain insight and grow.

Principle 4 is Diversity. Diversity is the recognition and appreciation of your team members' differences and similarities. It can help you tap into your team's combined intelligence and expertise to produce original and creative ideas.

To welcome and appreciate diversity, apply the following strategies:

1) Learn about your team members' origins, experiences, and opinions, and demonstrate attention and curiosity.

2) Respect and cherish your team members' perspectives and contributions, and avoid prejudices and biases.

3) Promote and support the expression and interchange of varied ideas and points of view, while avoiding groupthink and uniformity.

Accountability is the fourth guideline. Accountability refers to you and your team members' duty and dedication to your activities and results. It can assist you in improving your performance and quality, as well as meeting your promises and expectations.

You can use the following suggestions to encourage and exhibit accountability:

- Set clear and reasonable goals and expectations for yourself and your team members, and communicate them clearly and frequently.
- Track and assess your progress and outcomes, as well as provide and receive feedback and recognition.
- Recognize, address, and learn from your mistakes and shortcomings.
- Recognize and appreciate your accomplishments and victories, and share them with others.

Principle 6: Have faith. Trust is your and your team members' trust and believe in each other's abilities, intentions, and integrity. It can assist you in developing powerful and long-lasting connections, as well as improving collaboration and communication.

You can use the following techniques to create and retain trust:

- Be honest and straightforward with your team members, and avoid lying or withholding information.

- Be dependable and consistent with your team members, and keep your commitments and pledges.
- Show your team members respect and support, and avoid criticizing or blaming them.
- Share your opinions and feelings with your team members by being open and vulnerable.

By adhering to these standards and practices, you may foster a synergistic culture that not only increases production but also enhances the team experience. You may use your team's diversity and abilities to build a whole that is larger than the sum of its parts.

Synergizing is a strong habit that can lead to more productive and satisfying teamwork. It is about fostering a collaborative culture in which everyone feels appreciated and invested in the outcomes. You may lay the groundwork for productive and pleasurable teamwork by following the criteria of shared vision, mutual support, feedback, diversity, accountability, and trust.

CHAPTER EIGHT
SEEK FEEDBACK AND IMPROVE

Because it enables you to recognize your strengths and shortcomings, grow from your errors, and enhance your performance, feedback is crucial for productivity. You can get feedback from a variety of people, including your friends, mentors, co-workers, customers, and even yourself. But not every piece of input is equally worthwhile. You must look for constructive, actionable, and specific input.

Instead of making general or ambiguous remarks, specific feedback concentrates on a single area of your work. An example of specific comments might be, "Your presentation was well-structured and clear, but you could have used more visuals and examples to illustrate your points," as opposed to, "Your presentation was good." You can better grasp your strengths and areas for improvement when you receive specific feedback.

Feedback that is meant to support your development rather than discourage or condemn you is known as constructive feedback. An example of constructive criticism might be, "Your report contained some factual errors and grammatical mistakes, which affected your credibility and clarity," as opposed to, "Your report was terrible." Before turning in your work, be sure you have verified your sources." You may overcome obstacles and accomplish your goals with the aid of constructive criticism.

Feedback that offers specific recommendations on how to enhance your work instead of just highlighting issues is known as actionable feedback. An actionable feedback would be, for instance, "Your code has some logical errors and syntax errors, which cause it to crash," as opposed to "Your code is buggy". To locate and correct the mistakes, you ought to utilize a code editor and a debugger." Feedback that you can put to use helps you make the required improvements to your work.

You can develop the practice of asking for criticism and making improvements by paying attention to these pointers:

Seek out input on a frequent basis. Asking for input shouldn't be left until the end of a task or project. Throughout the process, get input from others so that you can make changes and advancements as needed. Aspects of your work that you would need comments on specifically include ideas, plans, methods, outcomes, or presentation.

Select your sources of input carefully. Ask those with appropriate experience, knowledge, and competence in your sector or domain for their opinions. Seek input from those who can provide you with frank and helpful criticism and who genuinely care about your wellbeing. Seek input on your work from a variety of sources to gain a range of viewpoints and insights.

Pay attention to criticism with an open mind. Remarks shouldn't be taken defensively or personally. Feedback is a tool to help you get better at what you do; it is not a measure of your value as a person. As you respectfully and curiously listen to criticism, make an effort to comprehend the viewpoint and intentions of the person providing it. Instead of debating or defending your work, raise questions and get any confusion or uncertainties cleared up.

React quickly to criticism. Don't discount or reject criticism; instead, see it as a chance to improve. Implement the recommendations that you agree with and respond to the comments you get. If there are comments that you disagree with, you can defend your position or get a second perspective. Monitor your development and outcomes, and assess the effects of your efforts.

We appreciate your feedback providers. Reward and express your gratitude to those who provide you with input, and respect their time and work. Tell them how you have improved your work using their feedback, and thank them for their input. Celebrate your successes together and let them know about your results and accomplishments.

The seventh habit of highly productive people is to continuously seek feedback and improve, as this leads to improved performance, knowledge, and skills. You can use feedback as an effective tool for productivity and development if you ask for specific, helpful, and actionable criticism and if you listen, respond, and express gratitude.

CHAPTER NINE
FREQUENTLY ASKED QUESTIONS

In this chapter, I will address some of the most often asked questions about the 7 habits of extraordinarily productive people. I hope that these responses will assist you in better understanding and applying the habits, as well as overcoming any hurdles or issues that you may have.

Q: What are the seven habits of highly productive people?

A: The following are the seven behaviors of highly productive people:

Connect their behaviors with their goals. This habit assists you in setting clear and realistic goals and organizing your work and time based on their relevance and urgency.

Concentrate on the consequences of their actions. This practice allows you to focus on your most critical work while avoiding or minimizing everything that could interrupt or divert your attention.

Optimize their efficiency. This habit assists you in overcoming procrastination and inertia, allowing you to execute things with quality and efficiency.

Think win-win situations. This habit allows you to track your progress and performance while also learning from your achievements and disappointments.

Understand to be understood. This practice aids in the maintenance of your physical and mental health, as well as the prevention of burnout and stress.

Synergize. This habit allows you to harness the power of collaboration and share your workload and obligations with others.

Ask for comments and make improvements. This practice allows you to improve your abilities, knowledge, and performance while also learning from feedback.

Q: How can I cultivate these habits?

A: Developing these behaviors necessitates constant practice and dedication. You can begin by taking the following steps:

Work on only one habit at a time. Instead than attempting to alter everything at once, concentrate on one habit that you wish to improve or master. This will assist you in avoiding overwhelm and confusion, as well as increasing your chances of success.

Understand the habit's benefits and drawbacks. Learn why the habit is necessary and beneficial to your productivity, as well as what potential challenges or issues you may face. This will assist you in motivating yourself and preparing for the habit shift.

Develop a precise and measurable habit goal. Define your goals for the habit and how you will track your progress and accomplishments. For example, if you want to cultivate the habit of planning and prioritizing, make a daily to-do list every morning and prioritize your chores based on priority and urgency.

Develop a habit strategy and schedule. Determine when, when, and how you will exercise the habit, as well as the resources or tools required. For example, if you want to build the habit of focusing and removing distractions, you could set out 90 minutes in the morning to work on your most essential assignment in a peaceful and comfortable environment, with your phone and notifications switched off.

Keep track of and reward your habits. Keep track of your habits and celebrate your accomplishments and milestones. For example, if you want to build the habit of taking action and finishing what you start, you could use a calendar or a journal to mark the days when you finished your duties, and then reward yourself with something you enjoy, such as a movie or a snack.

Reconsider and revise your habit. Evaluate your habit practice and determine what works and what does not. Change or improve your habit as needed, and seek criticism and help from others. If you want to create the habit of reviewing and reflecting, for example, you could use a weekly or monthly review template to examine your progress and performance and solicit comments from your co-workers or mentors.

Q: How long does it take for a habit to form?

A: There is no clear answer to this issue because different habits require varying amounts of time and work to acquire, based on factors such as your personality, motivation, surroundings, and previous habits. According to some research, it takes an average of 66 days to acquire a new habit. This means that you must constantly practice the habit for roughly two months before it becomes instinctive and natural to you. This is not a hard and fast rule, and you may require more or less time based on your condition and circumstances. The trick is to be patient and persistent, rather than giving up or becoming frustrated if you skip a day or make a mistake.

Q: What are some of the most typical problems or blunders people make while attempting to build habits?

A: The following are some of the most typical problems or blunders that people make when attempting to build habits:

Being unrealistic or overly optimistic. Setting unrealistic or ill-defined objectives, such as "I want to be more productive" or "I want to do everything," can lead to frustration and disappointment, as well as a loss of drive and confidence. Instead, develop SMART goals: Specific, Measurable, Achievable, Relevant, and Time-bound. Instead of saying, "I want to be more productive," say, "I want to finish my project by the end of the week."

Attempting to modify too many habits at the same time. Trying to acquire or adjust multiple habits at the same time, such as "I want to plan, focus, act, review, rest, collaborate, and seek feedback every day," can result in overwhelm and confusion, as well as a loss of focus and energy. Instead, pick one behavior to focus on at a time and master it before moving on to the next. This will assist you in avoiding confrontation and interference, as well as increasing your chances of success.

Relying solely on willpower or motivation. Without developing a supporting environment or system, relying on your willpower or drive to exercise your habit can lead to inconsistency and failure, as your willpower or motivation may fluctuate or decline over time. Instead, you should design a habit loop that has three components: a cue, a routine, and a reward. A cue, such as a time, a place, or an event, is a trigger that reminds you to exercise your habit. A routine is an action that you do as a habit, such as writing, reading, or exercising. A reward is a benefit you receive from engaging in your habit, such as satisfaction, pleasure, or acknowledgment. You can make your habit easier and more fun to practice by building a habit loop, as well as reinforce it in your brain.

Ignoring the significance of feedback and improvement. Ignoring or rejecting feedback from yourself or others, or neglecting to use it to improve your habit, can lead to stagnation and decline, as well as missed opportunities for learning and progress. Instead, seek precise, constructive, and practical feedback and listen to it with an open mind and a positive attitude. You should also act on the comments you get and put the suggestions you agree with into action. You may improve your abilities, knowledge, and performance and reach your goals faster and better by asking feedback and improving.

Q: How can I keep these habits going in the long run?

A: Long-term maintenance of these habits necessitates consistent practice and commitment. You may keep these practices going by following these suggestions:

Review and renew your objectives. Check in with your goals on a frequent basis to ensure that they are still relevant and important to you. If you have achieved or outgrown your old goals, you might set new or higher ones. You may maintain motivation and direction while avoiding complacency and boredom by examining and renewing your goals.

Change and challenge your habits. Experiment with new or different tools or resources, as well as new or different ways of practicing your habits. You can also make your habits more tough or complex, or add new or additional features to them. You may keep your interest and enthusiasm alive by challenging and diversifying your behaviors and avoiding monotony and routine.

Share and encourage your habits. Inform people about your habits and invite them to join or follow you. You can also join or form a community or a group of people who share your habits or goals in order to exchange ideas, experiences, and criticism. You may maintain accountability and responsibility while avoiding isolation and loneliness by sharing and supporting your behaviors.

CONCLUSION

Congratulations on completing this book! You now understand the seven habits of highly productive people and how they can help you do more with less time and effort. These are the habits:

Connect their behaviors with their goals. This habit assists you in setting clear and realistic goals and organizing your work and time based on their relevance and urgency.

Concentrate on the consequences of their actions. This practice allows you to focus on your most critical work while avoiding or minimizing everything that could interrupt or divert your attention.

Optimize their efficiency. This habit assists you in overcoming procrastination and inertia, allowing you to execute things with quality and efficiency.

Think win-win situations. This habit allows you to track your progress and performance while also learning from your achievements and disappointments.

Understand to be understood. This practice aids in the maintenance of your physical and mental health, as well as the prevention of burnout and stress.

Synergize. This habit allows you to harness the power of collaboration and share your workload and obligations with others.

Ask for comments and make improvements. This practice allows you to improve your abilities, knowledge, and performance while also learning from feedback.

These behaviors are beneficial not only to your job, but also to your personal and professional development. By implementing these habits, you may boost your productivity, creativity, and happiness, as well as achieve your goals faster and more effectively.

However, simply learning these habits is insufficient. You must constantly and efficiently implement them in your daily life. To do so, I recommend the following steps:

Begin small and easy. Instead of attempting to alter everything at once, focus on one habit at a time and master it before moving on to the next. Begin with the most relevant or easiest habit for you and practice it for at least 66 days, until it becomes routine and natural for you.

Make it enjoyable and rewarding. Consider these behaviors to be opportunities and benefits rather than obligations or burdens. Use gamification, imagery, or music to make your habit practice more pleasurable and gratifying. When you practice your habit or achieve your objective, reward yourself with something you enjoy, such as a compliment, a present, or a break.

Keep track of and evaluate your progress. Use tools and processes to document and analyze your habit practice and results rather than relying on your recollection or intuition. You can, for example, track your habit frequency, duration, and quality using a calendar, a journal, or an app. You can also utilize indicators like as analytics, feedback, or testimonials to assess the impact and outcome of your habit.

Seek assistance and accountability. Participate in your habit journey with others rather than doing it alone. Share your habit goals and plans with your family, friends, or co-workers, and invite others to join, follow, or remind you. You can also join or form a community or a group of people who share your habits or goals in order to exchange ideas, experiences, and criticism.

Continue to study and improve. Strive for perfection rather than good enough. Maintain your knowledge of the most recent research and trends in productivity and habits. Experiment with fresh or alternative ways of carrying out your habits and evaluate their usefulness and efficiency. Seek and use feedback from yourself and others to improve your behaviors and results.

I hope this book has motivated and inspired you to be more productive and successful. I also hope you have had as much fun reading this book as I have had creating it. Thank you for your time and consideration, and best wishes on your productivity path. Remember that productivity is a journey, not a destination. And you have the ability to make it a fantastic one. Good luck with your habit formation!

www.ingramcontent.com/pod-product-compliance
Lightning Source LLC
Chambersburg PA
CBHW062240290526
45794CB00006B/2355